my first
Camping
ABC
Picture Book

This book belongs to:

_____

A is for
Animals

B is for
Binoculars

C is for

Compass

D is for
Day Pack

E is for
Evergreen

F is for
Fire

G is for
Guitar

H is for
Hiking Boots

I is for
Ice Chest

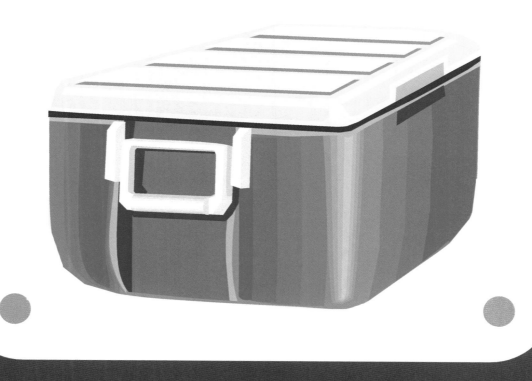

J is for
Jacket

K is for
Knife

L is for
Lantern

M is for
Mountains

N is for
National Park

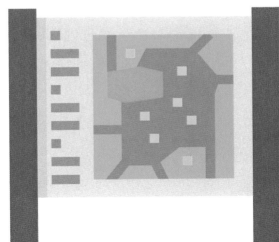

O is for
Owl

P is for
Path

Q is for
Quail

R is for
RV

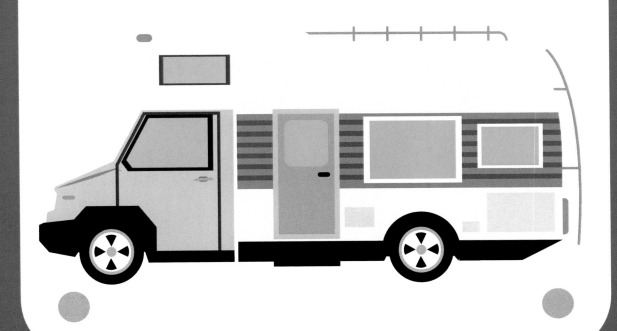

S is for
S'Mores

T is for
Tent

U is for
Under the Stars

V is for
Vehicles

W is for
Waterfall

X is for
XO XO

Y is for
Youth

Z is for
Zip Up

Happy Camping!

Made in United States
Orlando, FL
14 June 2025

62118302R00019